AF599458

THE WORLD OF PHYSICS

# MATTER & ENERGY

by
Tom Jackson

Minneapolis, Minnesota

**Credits**

Cover and title page, © NiPlot/iStock; 3, © Dmitry/Adobe Stock; 4MR, © Yuri Arcurs/Adobe Stock; 4BL, © D–VISIONS/Shutterstock; 4–5, © stnazkul/iStock; 5BR, © Eric Bordelon/NASA; 6ML, © Aygul Sarvarova/Shutterstock; 6BL, © Sirocco/Shutterstock; 6–7, © Stock Rocket/Shutterstock; 7TL, © National Portrait Gallery London/Wikimedia; 8MR, © KenAge/Shutterstock; 8BR, © Library of Congress/Wikimedia; 8–9, © nobeastsofierce/Shutterstock; 9BR, © Lukasz Pawel Szczepanski/Shutterstock; 10MR, © StockCanarias/Shutterstock; 10BL, © Gene Tewksbury/Wikimedia; 10–11, © Simon Balson/Alamy; 11TR, © Artsiom P/Shutterstock; 12ML, © hedgehog94/Shutterstock; 12BR, © Maridav/Shutterstock; 12–13, © Jake Lyell/Alamy Stock Photo; 13BL, © Public Domain/Wikimedia; 14ML, © Bettmann Archive/Getty Images; 14BR, © COMPUSIR/Adobe Stock; 15, © aradaphotography/Adobe Stock; 15BL, © Public Domain/Wikimedia; 16MR, © BlueRingMedia/Shutterstock; 16BL, © Tomas Ragina/Shutterstock; 16–17, © Angelaoblak/Shutterstock; 17BL, © Public Domain/Wikimedia; 18ML, © Tada Images/Adobe Stock; 18MR, © Kzenon/Adobe Stock; 18BL, © Public Domain/Wikimedia; 18–19, © txking/Shutterstock; 20ML, © Mike Flippo/Shutterstock; 20BR, © Friends Stock/Shutterstock; 20–21, © Lianys/Shutterstock; 21TL, © Colport/Alamy Stock Photo; 22MR, © StoryTime Studio/Shutterstock; 22BL, © PeopleImages.com – Yuri A/Shutterstock; 22–23, © Monkey Business Images/Shutterstock; 23BL, © Pictorial Press Ltd/Alamy Stock Photo; 24ML, © P Greenwood Photography/Shutterstock; 24BL, © Public Domain/Wikimedia; 24–25, © RobSt/Shutterstock; 25MR, © sirtravelalot/Shutterstock; 26MR, © OSweetNature/Shutterstock; 26CR, © Milan Sommer/Shutterstock; 26BR, © Standret/Shutterstock; 26–27, © marilook/Shutterstock; 27BL Public Domain/Wikimedia; 28MR, © Johan Swanepoel/Shutterstock; 28BL, © New Africa/Shutterstock; 28–29, © sciencephotos/Alamy Stock Photo; 29BL, © Public Domain/Wikimedia; 30MR, © Pixel B/Shutterstock; 30BL, © Anatoliy Sadovskiy/Shutterstock and, © photka/Adobe Stock; 30–31, © JoeSAPhotos/Shutterstock; 31BL, © Public Domain/Wikimedia; 32ML, © Billion Photos/Shutterstock; 32BR, © VectorMine/Shutterstock; 32–33, © NewSs/Shutterstock; 33BL, © Public Domain/Wikimedia; 34MR, © VectorMine/Shutterstock; 34BL, © Public Domain/Wikimedia; 34–35, © Vershinin89/Shutterstock; 35TR, © petrroudny43/Shutterstock; 36ML, © Ferenc Szelepcsenyi/Alamy Stock Photo; 36BR, © Andrewshots/Shutterstock; 36–37, © Lappo Alexander/Shutterstock; 37BL, © Public Domain/Wikimedia; 38MR, © huntingSHARK/Shutterstock; 38BL, © huntingSHARK/Shutterstock; 38–39, © ronstik/Shutterstock; 39TL, © Science History Images/Alamy Stock Photo; 40MR, © Dn Br/Shutterstock; 40ML, © Rainbow06/Shutterstock; 40BL, © Public Domain/Wikimedia; 40–41, © Grzegorz Czapski/Shutterstock; 41TR, © Peter Sobolev/Shutterstock; 42MR, © VALENTIN FLAURAUD/Getty Images; 42BL, © davelogan/iStock; 42, © Reid Wiseman/NASA; 44, © Maridav/Shutterstock; 45TL, © Artsiom P/Shutterstock; 45B, © txking/Shutterstock; 47B, © Vershinin89/Shutterstock

**Bearport Publishing Company Product Development Team**

Publisher: Jen Jenson; Director of Product Development: Spencer Brinker; Managing Editor: Allison Juda; Editor: Cole Nelson; Associate Editor: Naomi Reich; Associate Editor: Tiana Tran; Art Director: Colin O'Dea; Designer: Kim Jones; Designer: Kayla Eggert; Product Development Specialist: Owen Hamlin

**Statement on Usage of Generative Artificial Intelligence**

Bearport Publishing remains committed to publishing high-quality nonfiction books. Therefore, we restrict the use of generative AI to ensure accuracy of all text and visual components pertaining to a book's subject. See BearportPublishing.com for details.

Library of Congress Cataloging-in-Publication Data is available at www.loc.gov or upon request from the publisher.

ISBN: 979-8-89232-896-8 (hardcover)
ISBN: 979-8-89232-926-2 (ebook)



For more information, write to Bearport Publishing, 5357 Penn Avenue South, Minneapolis, MN 55419.

# Contents

# The Building Blocks of the Universe

Everything we see is made of matter and filled with energy. All matter that we know of in the universe is made of atoms and atomic particles that are too small to see and that hold some amount of energy. Some of this energy keeps atoms together. But energy can also be released as heat, light, radiation, or electricity when matter goes through certain changes. Throughout history, humans have found many ways to harness the energy within matter for creative and destructive ends.

## Energy

Energy is the ability to do work. It can come in many different forms, such as the energy of movement, heat, or sound. Energy can be changed, or transformed, from one form into another. However, it can never be created or destroyed. Everything that happens in the universe, from a bouncing ball to an exploding star, requires energy.

A runner's muscles use electrical currents to contract and expand, turning potential energy into kinetic energy.

The Large Hadron Collider accelerates subatomic particles over 16.7 miles (27 km) before smashing them together.

## Matter

Matter is made up of tiny building blocks called atoms, which are in turn made from even smaller subatomic particles. To study matter, researchers use huge machines called particle accelerators that smash subatomic particles together at enormous speeds.

## Studying the Universe

Scientists who study physics are called physicists. Physics is the science of matter—the stuff from which everything is made—and the energy that moves and transforms matter. Understanding physics allows us to explain how everything else works.

Some physicists are rocket scientists. They study how to burn fuel to create enough energy to lift a spacecraft out of Earth's atmosphere.

# What Is Matter?

Matter is anything that takes up space and has mass. All matter is made of tiny particles called atoms. Your body, your home, trees, oceans, rocks, and everything else on planet Earth are made of matter. All matter, and in some cases empty space, is filled with different kinds of energy. This energy does not take up space or have mass, but changes in energy can cause matter to change its form or state.

The most familiar matter that changes between solid, liquid, and gas is water. On Earth, it is solid as ice, liquid as water, and a gas as steam.

## States of Matter

Matter exists in three main states—solid, liquid, and gas. The state is the result of how atoms move within the matter. Matter changes state as it becomes hotter or colder. In a cold solid, the atoms are arranged into a fixed shape and volume. Solids melt into liquids as they warm up. Liquids have a fixed volume but no fixed shape. Heating a liquid until it boils makes a gas, which has neither a fixed shape nor a fixed volume.

## Matter and Energy

When matter is heated, the heat energy makes its atoms vibrate. As matter cools, its atoms move less. Matter can also lose or gain energy in a chemical change. A chemical change rearranges the atoms into different substances. For example, burning a log changes it from wood into smoke, gas, and ash.

An explosion is a rapid chemical change that transforms the physical nature of matter. Some matter is converted to smoke or gases. A lot of energy is released as heat.



**DID YOU KNOW?** There is a fourth state of matter called plasma. It can be created when a gas gets very hot or is affected by electricity. The sun is made of plasma.

HALL OF FAME
John Dalton
1766–1844
The idea of matter being made of atoms dates back to ancient Greece. British scientist John Dalton introduced modern atomic theory in 1803. He suggested that atoms of different types combine to make different substances. He noted that they always combine in the same proportions to make the new substance.
Matter can be pushed and pulled by forces. These forces can make matter move and change shape.
Although we cannot see it, we are surrounded by matter all the time in the form of gases in the air.
The atoms that make up matter are made of smaller particles called protons, neutrons, and electrons.

# Inside Atoms

There are 118 chemical elements. These are simple substances such as carbon and gold. The elements are the ingredients of all matter. Each element has its own unique type of atom. Atoms differ in the number of subatomic particles they contain.

## Smaller Particles

We used to think atoms were indivisible, meaning they could not be broken down. However, now physicists know atoms are made up of smaller subatomic particles. Each atom has a nucleus in the middle. Within it, there are roughly equal numbers of protons and neutrons. Electrons whiz around the nucleus. The width of an atom is more than 10,000 times the width of its nucleus, so most of an atom's volume is empty space. The neutrons and protons themselves are made of even smaller particles, called quarks. There are three quarks in each neutron or proton.

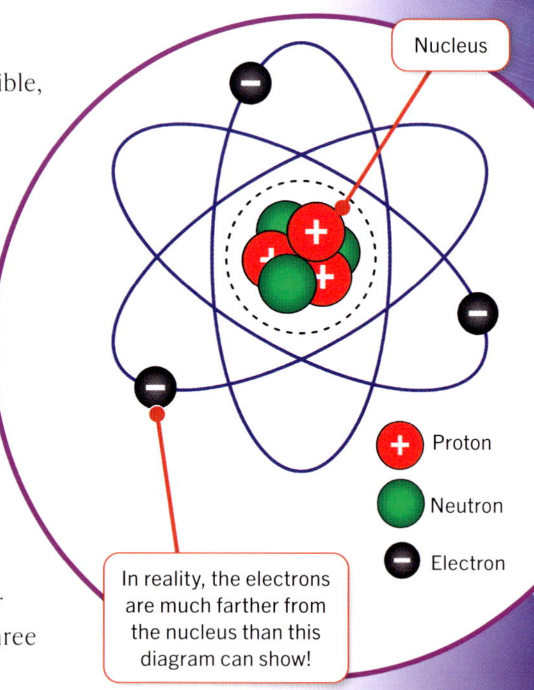

**HALL OF FAME**

### Ernest Rutherford
### 1871–1937

Ernest Rutherford became one of the first atomic physicists. In 1911, this scientist from New Zealand led the team that discovered that atoms have a compact nucleus and a lot of empty space. They found that the positive charge of an atom is concentrated in its nucleus. In 1997, an element with 104 protons was named Rutherfordium in his honor.



**DID YOU KNOW?** An atom is approximately 0.2 to 0.5 nanometers across. A nanometer is a billionth of a meter.

An atom that has the same number of electrons and protons has a neutral charge. But ions, or atoms that have gained more electrons than usual, carry a negative charge.

Electrons have a negative charge and move around the outside of the atom. This balances out the positive charge of the protons in the nucleus.

A proton is 1,836 times heavier than an electron.

## Nuclear Reactions

Actions that disrupt the nucleus, called nuclear reactions, release a lot of energy. The most powerful of these is nuclear fusion, in which two nuclei are smashed together so they merge into one. This creates a different element. The sun's heat and light come from fusion deep inside the star.

One day, nuclear fusion could be an abundant source of clean power. For now, we get the power of nuclear fusion from the sun in the form of solar power.

# Weight and Mass

Weight and mass are often used interchangeably, but they have different meanings. Mass is a measure of how much matter is in an object. That object's weight is the force of gravity pulling on it. Two objects of the same mass would weigh the same amount on Earth, but if one was on the moon it would weigh much less than the other. But the masses of both objects would still be the same.

The mass of these weights is a fixed amount, a measure of the amount of matter in them. That never changes—even in space.

## Making Measurements

Weight is measured using scales that identify the force of gravity pulling down on an object. Mass is measured by how much an object will resist moving. When floating in space, an object does not push down on scales at all and so it is weightless, but since it has mass it still needs enough of a pushing force to get it moving—and to stop it again.

Electronic scales measure weight by how much an object presses down on a pad inside.

HALL OF FAME

### Andrea Ghez
### Born 1965

Andrea Ghez is an American astronomer who discovered the most massive thing in our galaxy. Ghez showed that there is a black hole in the middle of the Milky Way called Sagittarius A*. Ghez used big telescopes to watch how the gravity from the black hole made nearby stars move very fast. She used those speeds to calculate the pull of gravity from the black hole, which told her that Sagittarius A* had a mass four million times that of the sun!



**DID YOU KNOW?** The pilots of fast fighter jets feel extra weight as they accelerate through a turn. The force that causes this extra weight is called a g-force.

## Weightless in Space

Astronauts on the International Space Station (ISS) have no weight, since they are in constant free fall around the planet. Still, they need to monitor their mass to make sure they stay healthy. This is measured using a special device that calculates how much force is needed to move their bodies against a spring with a known resistance.

An astronaut in space is weightless but not massless.

A weightlifter has to create a force stronger than gravity to get the weight off the ground and above their head.

**The weight of this bar depends on the force of gravity pulling it down to the ground. On Jupiter, where the gravity is stronger, its weight would be nearly three times greater than on Earth!**

# Doing Work

To a physicist, the term *work* has a very particular meaning. Work is the transfer of energy from one object to another. It can happen only when a force is applied. Scientists use units of joules to measure how much work is being done.

Exercise makes us hot because our muscles warm up as they work hard.

## Heating Up

When work is done, some of the energy is always transferred in the form of heat. That heat energy leaks away into nearby particles. This leaking of energy is due to a process called entropy. Because of entropy, energy within and emitted by matter tends to spread out throughout the universe.

## Falling Down

The water in this waterfall is doing work as it gushes downward. At the top, the water has potential energy. This is energy it has as a result of its position or state, which can be converted to another form. When gravity causes the water to fall over the cliff, the water's potential energy is converted into kinetic energy in the form of motion.

The water is a little bit hotter at the bottom of the waterfall because some of the kinetic energy is converted into heat energy.



**DID YOU KNOW?** The average human body uses about 10,000 kilojoules in 24 hours. A kilojoule is equal to 1,000 joules.

**HALL OF FAME**

### James Joule 1818–1889

The unit of energy, the joule, is named after the British scientist James Joule. He wanted to show that heat and motion are related forms of energy. In the 1840s, Joule performed a famous experiment in which he used a falling weight to spin a stirrer in a tank of water. He showed that dropping the weight over and over again made the water gradually get warmer.

# Conservation of Energy and Mass

When a candle is burned, the wax does not just disappear. Instead, some of the wax's matter changes state from a solid to a gas. The rest of the candle is turned into energy in the form of heat. This is because mass and energy can never be created or destroyed. But under the right conditions, any object with mass can be converted into energy. Scientists call this the law of conservation of energy and mass.

John Ernst Worrell Keely claimed to have invented an engine that harnessed a mysterious force called interatomic ether to create endless energy. It was later revealed to simply run off compressed air.

## Perpetual Motion

Many people have tried to create a perpetual motion machine, or a machine that can run forever. Sadly, perpetual motion machines are impossible according to known physics. This is because any time energy is transferred, at least a small amount is lost through friction and heat. Eventually, a machine loses energy and stops.

## Oxidation

When metal rusts, it may seem to lose mass and get smaller. Actually, the oxygen in the air is taking electrons from the iron, forming a chemical substance called rust. The same amount of matter still exists, but it has changed into a new substance.

Salt in sea water can make iron oxidize and create rust faster.

**DID YOU KNOW?** With his theory of relativity, Einstein showed that energy can be converted into matter. But it takes a lot of energy to create a small amount of matter.

Candles use a process of oxidation to combine vaporized wax with oxygen in the air. The chemical reaction releases thermal energy, keeping the flame burning.

The flame of a candle transfers its thermal energy to the solid wax below. As the atoms in the wax move faster, it changes state from solid to liquid. The liquid wax moves up the wick and is burned by the flame.

Though a candle gets smaller as it burns, its matter and energy have not disappeared. The chemical energy is released as thermal energy in the flame. The flame has converted the solid wax and wick into smoke, vapor, and ash.

**HALL OF FAME**

**Nicolas Léonard Sadi Carnot**

**1796–1832**

In the 1820s, this French soldier and engineer investigated how steam engines worked. What he discovered could be used to explain how all engines work and how energy is transferred. Carnot is sometimes called the father of thermodynamics, a field of physics that deals with heat, work, and energy.

# Thermal Energy

Thermal energy is energy in the form of heat. It is held by the atoms and molecules in a substance. As the atoms within a material gain thermal energy, they vibrate faster, and the material becomes hotter. Thermal energy is always on the move. Through entropy, this energy spreads out from hot things to colder things until eventually everything is the same temperature.

## Heat Transfer

There are three ways thermal energy moves—conduction, convection, and radiation. Conduction happens in solids as atoms jostle one another. Convection is caused by warm liquids and gases rising up through colder ones. As hot material cools and falls again, it is replaced by newly heated matter rising, setting up a current that spreads heat. Radiation carries the energy as invisible heat rays, called infrared waves.

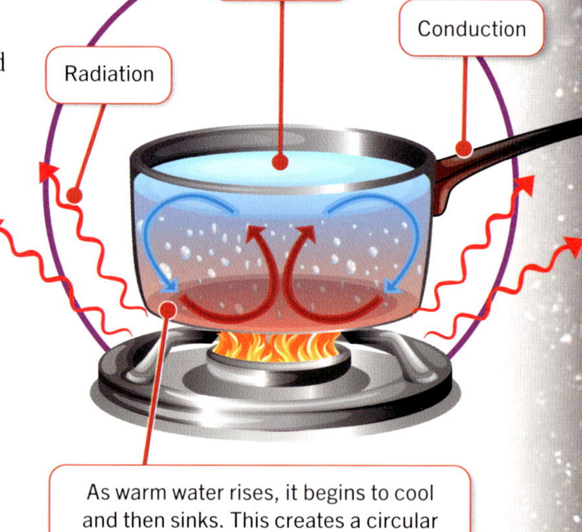


As warm water rises, it begins to cool and then sinks. This creates a circular current that moves heat around.

Temperature scales fix an upper and lower point and divide the gap between into units called degrees. This thermometer shows that the temperature is at the freezing point of water, or 32 degrees Fahrenheit (0°C).

## Taking the Temperature

Temperature is a measure of the average kinetic energy of the particles in a substance. Temperature is not a measure of the total energy in the material. An iceberg, for example, contains many more atoms than a hot spark coming from a fire, so it carries much more energy in total. However, the spark is at a much higher temperature. Thermometers are used to measure temperature.

HALL OF FAME

**Lord Kelvin**

**1824–1907**

Born William Thomson, the Scottish physicist Lord Kelvin worked on heat and other forms of energy. He transformed our understanding of physics and helped create new technologies, such as refrigeration and telecommunications. Kelvin discovered that the minimum possible temperature, or absolute zero, is –459°F (–273°C). This is the temperature at which matter has the smallest possible amount of thermal energy. It is now known as 0 Kelvins, with each Kelvin equivalent to 1°C.

**DID YOU KNOW?** Half the energy from the sun is in the form of invisible infrared heat waves. Light makes up only 40 percent of the sun's energy that reaches Earth.

# Kinetic Energy

The energy of motion is called kinetic energy. Kinetic energy is most obvious when it is making big things such as cars and trains move. The moon, Earth, the sun—and all other objects in the universe—are moving as well. There is kinetic energy even at the smallest scale with the movement of atoms. The amount of kinetic energy an object has depends on both its mass and its velocity.

## Speed and Safety

As an object's velocity increases, so does its kinetic energy—but not by the same amount. When the speed of an object doubles, its kinetic energy increases four times. To move at twice the speed, an object needs four times as much energy. This is why speed limits on roads are important. Even small increases in speed mean that vehicles are moving with much more energy and can do more damage in a collision.

## Energy Transfer

When one moving object collides with another, the faster object transfers kinetic energy to the slower one. As well as being linked to velocity, kinetic energy is proportional to the mass of the moving body. So if two objects are moving at the same speed, the more massive one always has more energy. How much energy is transferred in collisions depends on the angle of the collision and how hard or flexible the objects are.

A blocker on a football team absorbs the kinetic energy of their opponent, stopping them.

HALL OF FAME

**Émilie du Châtelet**
**1706–1749**

The French scientist and mathematician Émilie du Châtelet linked the idea of kinetic energy to mass and velocity. She also helped to explain that energy of any kind is never made or destroyed, but transformed into other types. Much of du Châtelet's work is found in her translation of Isaac Newton's writings, to which she added her own ideas and improvements.

**DID YOU KNOW?** The word *kinetic* comes from the Greek word for movement. The word *cinema* has the same origin, because it is a place with moving pictures.

# Potential Energy

While kinetic energy is concerned with motion of all kinds, potential energy describes how energy can be stored by objects in different ways. This energy is released when work is done to objects that hold potential energy. Potential energy is always there, even when the object seems to be doing nothing. It can be released when the conditions are right.

To recharge a battery, an electric current is used to push charged particles apart to create a store of potential energy. When the battery is used, that potential energy is released.

## Electrical Potential

One form of potential energy is electrical potential energy. This is the energy stored in batteries. It is created whenever a difference in electrical charge is created, where positive charges and negative charges are kept separated. To rebalance that charge and release the electrical potential energy, a circuit is closed allowing electrons to flow in a current.

## Elastic Potential

Some solid materials will deform, or change shape, when a force is applied to them. Permanent changes are called plastic deformations. Energy is not stored in these new shapes. Temporary changes are called elastic deformations. These shapes will spring back to normal when the force is released. The energy stored in a stretched material is called elastic potential energy. This kind of energy makes balls bounce and is used in spring-loaded and windup devices.

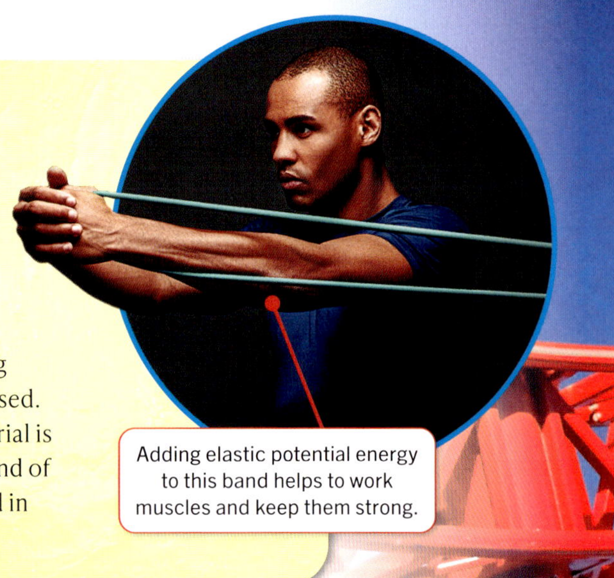

Adding elastic potential energy to this band helps to work muscles and keep them strong.



**DID YOU KNOW?** Rivers flow due to water's gravitational potential energy. Rain falls high on mountains, and the water is pulled downhill by gravity.

**HALL OF FAME**

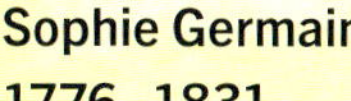

## Sophie Germain
## 1776–1831

As a woman growing up at the end of the eighteenth century, Sophie Germain was not allowed to study at a university. Instead, she wrote to many of the world's best scientists and helped them with their projects. In 1816, she won a grand prize given by the Paris Academy of Sciences for discovering how elastic solids worked. She was the first woman to be honored by the Paris Academy.

The riders on a roller coaster feel the sudden release of gravitational potential energy. After being lifted slowly to the top of a hill, riders then roll down the other side under the pull of gravity.

It takes a lot of work to push a roller coaster car up to this point. That work is converted into gravitational potential energy, which is released as the cars roll down the other side.

Gravity is making the cars accelerate as if they were in free fall through the air. The curved track slows the cars down gradually.

# Other Types of Energy

One of the main laws of physics is the conservation of energy. This law says that energy is never created or destroyed. Instead, it is transformed from one type of energy into another. In addition to motion, heat, and potential energy, there are several other kinds of energy.

## Electrical Energy

Most modern machines are powered using electrical energy. This is a flow of energy that is carried by a current of electrons. A heater is a very simple electrical machine. The flow of electrons pushes on atoms in a wire, converting their electrical energy into heat and, perhaps, visible light. Electric motors use magnets to create forces that make moving parts spin.

The microchips inside a computer are powered by electricity. They use the energy to perform calculations and execute instructions.

A megaphone uses electricity to wobble a cone back and forth very fast. That wobble creates a loud sound wave.

## Sound Energy

Sound is a wave of pressure that moves through the air. It is a kind of kinetic energy because the sound wave is moving the air molecules, causing them to spread apart and then squeeze together. Sound waves are created by the kinetic energy from other materials being transferred to the air. Loud sounds contain more energy than quiet ones.

HALL OF FAME

**Laura Bassi**
**1711–1778**

Born in what is now Bologna, Italy, Laura Bassi became the second woman in the world to earn a PhD, or doctorate degree. She was also the first woman to have a paid job as a teacher at Bologna's university, where she taught physics. Bassi studied electricity and became the main researcher in the physics department at the university.

**DID YOU KNOW?** Thinking takes energy. Your brain uses 20 percent of the energy your body needs each day.

# Power

Power is a measure of how quickly work is done, or how quickly energy is transferred from one object to another. For example, it takes the same amount of work for two swimmers of the same mass to swim a length of a pool, but a more powerful swimmer can do that work in less time.

This immensely powerful truck can move a very large load in a short amount of time.

## Watts

Power is measured with a unit called the watt, named after inventor and engineer James Watt. One watt is equal to 1 joule of energy transferred in 1 second. Most of our appliances at home have a power rating expressed in watts. This tells us how much energy they will use up. A machine with a lower power rating saves energy but might take longer to do the job.

The brightness of light bulbs is measured in watts. Stadium floodlights are around 10,000 times more powerful than the lights in your home.

HALL OF FAME

### James Watt
### 1736–1819

The Scottish engineer James Watt is known for his work on the steam engine, improving the efficiency of earlier designs. Before Watt, steam engines used a lot of fuel but were not very powerful. Watt's engines were large and powerful and were meant to be used in factories and mines. Later inventors made smaller engines for ships and trains.

## Using Power

A machine can be more powerful than a human body. This means one machine can do the work of many people. Early machines were compared to the strength and power of horses, which were used to haul heavy loads. That's why the original unit of power was horsepower. Today, the power of cars and other vehicles is sometimes still measured in horsepower. One horsepower is about 746 watts.

This truck is a complex machine that uses several kinds of simple machines to do work efficiently, such as wheels, levers, and pulleys.

This forklift can lift more weight than a person can. It can do it faster and go higher, too.

The dump truck uses powerful pistons to push up the load so that it slides off the back.

**DID YOU KNOW?** The most powerful rocket engine ever built, the F-1 engine that launched NASA's Saturn V rocket, had a power rating of 160 million horsepower.

# Radioactivity

Many atoms are stable and stay the same forever. But some large atoms have so many protons and neutrons that the nucleus tends to fall apart. The process of unstable atoms coming apart is called radioactivity. Radioactivity releases particles and energy that can be used in medicine and as a source of power.

## Radioactive Decay

Radioactive elements change through a process called radioactive decay. In these elements, the unstable nucleus pushes out particles to make itself more stable. Changing the number of protons in the nucleus transforms an atom from one element to another. For example, uranium atoms decay into thorium atoms. This process of decay stops when an atom reaches a stable form.

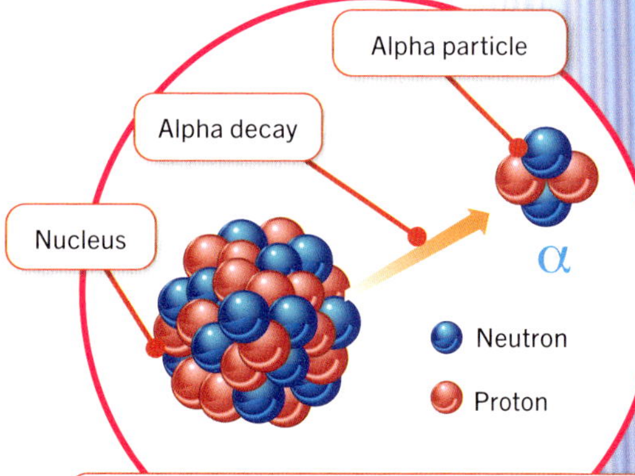


Alpha decay happens when the nucleus throws out two protons and two neutrons, called an alpha particle. In beta decay, the nucleus releases an electron, changing a neutron to a proton.

## Dangers of Radiation

Radioactive substances are dangerous and must be handled with care, because the energy released by decay can damage living cells. People who work with radioactive material must wear protective suits to block these particles. As well as alpha and beta particles, decay releases high-energy radiation, such as X-rays and gamma rays. These can be blocked by thick metal and concrete.

These symbols warn that radioactive substances are present in the area. Safety equipment should be used.

**HALL OF FAME**

### Marie Curie
### 1867–1934

Curie, a Polish physicist working in France, came up with the term *radioactivity*. She discovered several rare radioactive elements that are made when uranium in naturally occurring minerals decays. Curie became the first female member of the teaching faculty at the University of Paris. She later developed X-ray machines and set up a research center to study how radioactivity could be used in medicine.

**DID YOU KNOW?** Bananas emit tiny amounts of radioactivity, but they are completely safe to eat. You would have to eat 10 million bananas in one meal to get a dangerous dose.

# What Is Electricity?

Electricity is a form of energy that results from particles having a charge. When charged particles move in a stream, or current, electrical energy flows and can be used to do work. Electricity is an important source of power for technology, such as computers, heating, and lights. Electricity is widespread in the natural world, too. For example, electrical charges carried in your nerves make your muscles move.

## Moving Charge

Matter can have a positive or negative electrical charge, depending on the number of electrons present in each atom. Extra electrons give matter a negative charge. Two objects with the same charge repel each other, but opposite charges attract each other. The attraction between a negative and a positive charge is what pulls electricity along, making a current flow through a cable or other medium.

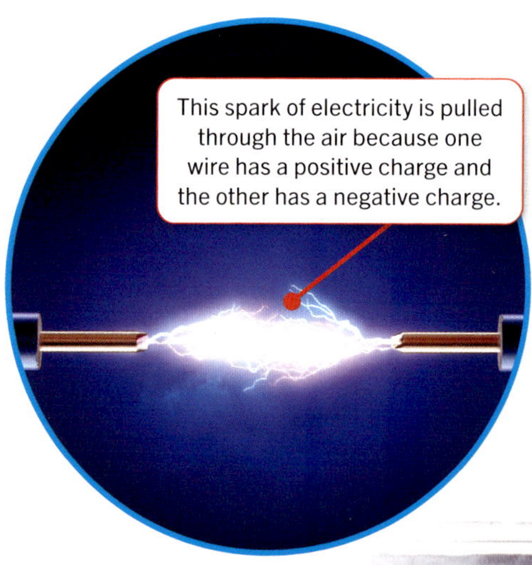

This spark of electricity is pulled through the air because one wire has a positive charge and the other has a negative charge.

Food mixers use electricity to spin sharp blades at high speeds to cut food into smaller chunks.

## Electrical Energy

Electrically powered devices use the energy of flowing electricity to do work, transforming it into another kind of energy. A heater or oven converts the electrical energy into thermal energy, while an electric car uses the energy to move. Many of these devices need a constant flow of electricity to keep working.

**HALL OF FAME**

### Nikola Tesla
### 1856–1943

The inventor and electrical engineer Nikola Tesla was born in Serbia but moved to America as a young man. He invented many electrical devices, including an electric motor, a wireless lighting system, a remote control that worked by radio, a vertical-take-off plane, and a so-called death ray. He also investigated X-rays and radio waves. Despite his many ideas, Tesla struggled to find money to fund his inventions, and most were never produced commercially.

**DID YOU KNOW?** The word *electricity* comes from the ancient Greek word for amber. Early scientists found that rubbing pieces of amber together produced sparks.

# Electromagnetism

Electromagnetism is one of the basic forces in the universe. It helps hold matter together and also produces electricity, magnetism, and light. All particles have an electric charge. They can be positive, negative, or neutral. Atoms that gain or lose electrons create an electromagnetic field around them. This field attracts opposite charges to it and repels similar charges.

## Light Radiation

Visible light, infrared light, radio waves, and X-rays are all forms of electromagnetic radiation. When electrons in an atom give out energy, they release a burst of light or another form of radiation. When that radiation hits another atom, it might be absorbed by an electron or reflected off again.

A laser is an instrument that can produce a powerful beam of light. The word *laser* stands for the scientific term that explains how a laser beam is produced: light amplification by stimulated emission of radiation.

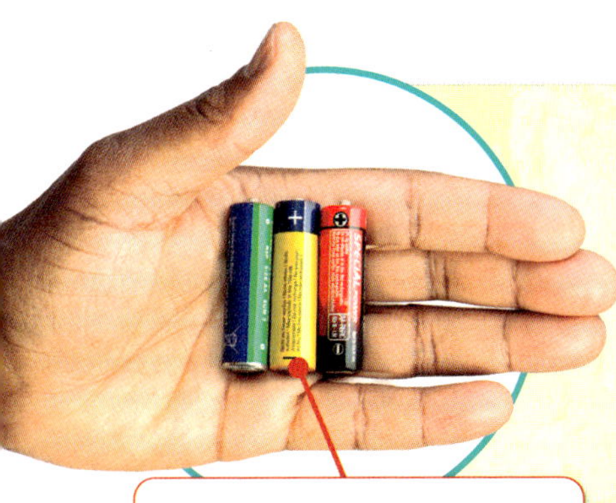

Batteries use chemical reactions to produce electric currents.

## Electric Currents

Electricity is a flow of charged particles—most often electrons. The electrons move from an area where there are many electrons to a place where there are fewer. Batteries and other sources of electricity keep the current flowing by continually adding more electrons at one end and removing them from the other.



**DID YOU KNOW?** While the force of electromagnetism is many trillions of times stronger than gravity, it is still more than 100 times weaker than the strong nuclear force.

The body's motion is powered by electromagnetic forces in the muscles. Charged particles called ions move through the muscle cells, making them change shape and contract the muscle.

The electromagnetic force helps keep atoms separated from one another. It pushes an atom's outermost electrons away from those of nearby atoms. This is why a baseball bounces off a bat instead of going through it.

The electromagnetic force helps hold atoms together, keeping the negatively charged electrons bound to the positively charged nucleus.

**HALL OF FAME**

## Hans Christian Ørsted
## 1777–1851

Danish scientist Hans Christian Ørsted discovered the link between electricity and magnetism, and thus he created a new area of physics called electromagnetism. Ørsted discovered that the magnetic needle of a compass swings toward a wire carrying an electric current, but then swings back to point north when the current is turned off. In 1820, he published his finding that an electric current produces a magnetic field around the wire through which it travels.

# Conductors and Insulators

Electricity requires electrons to flow freely inside a material. Conductors are materials that carry—or conduct—electricity well. This is because they have plenty of free electrons inside that can move around. Insulators are the opposite. They are materials that block or slow down the movement of electricity.

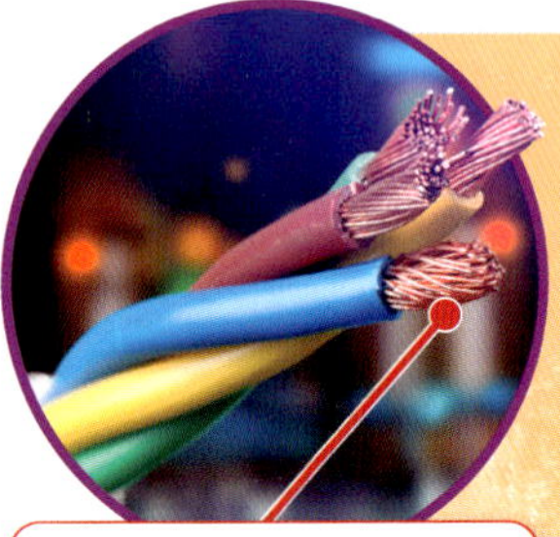

The electricity in wires can be powerful enough to injure or kill people. Do not touch a cable if you can see the metal inside.

## Live Wires

Electrical cables are made from a combination of conductors and insulators. The central part is composed of metal wires, often made of copper, which is an excellent conductor. The electricity flows easily through this metal. Around these wires is a flexible plastic coating. Plastic is a very good insulator, and it ensures that none of the electrical energy in the copper leaks out of the wires before it reaches its destination.

## Carriers and Blockers

All metals conduct electricity because they have many free electrons. Copper, gold, and silver are better conductors than most metals. Sea water is also an effective conductor because it contains dissolved salt in the water. This salt releases charged particles called ions that can carry electricity. Insulators are nonmetal substances, such as plastic and glass. Their electrons are locked in place and do not form a current to carry an electrical energy.

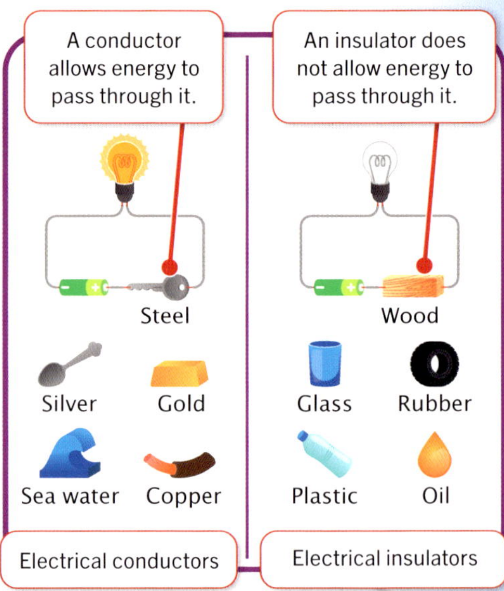




**DID YOU KNOW?** A superconductor is a material that conducts electricity without losing any energy at all. However, superconductors work only when they are very cold.

**HALL OF FAME**

## Stephen Gray
## 1666–1736

Stephen Gray, a British cloth-dyer-turned-scientist, began experimenting with electrical charges and conductors after noticing an attractive force between some of his glass bottles and pieces of cloth. He found that the charge from these glass bottles could be conducted through metals and some threads but it was blocked by silk.

# Current

Electricity can be static or flow as a current. Static electricity exists when there is an imbalance of electrical charge on a surface. If the surface touches a material that can carry away the extra electrons, a spark appears as the charge is instantly rebalanced between the surface and the material. An electric current forms when a difference in charge is maintained, so electrons flow constantly.

### Moving Electrons

As electrons move through a metal wire, they carry their negative charge with them. This causes a positive charge, or current, to move in the opposite direction. So, even though electrons move from the negative end of a battery to the positive end, the current moves from positive to negative.

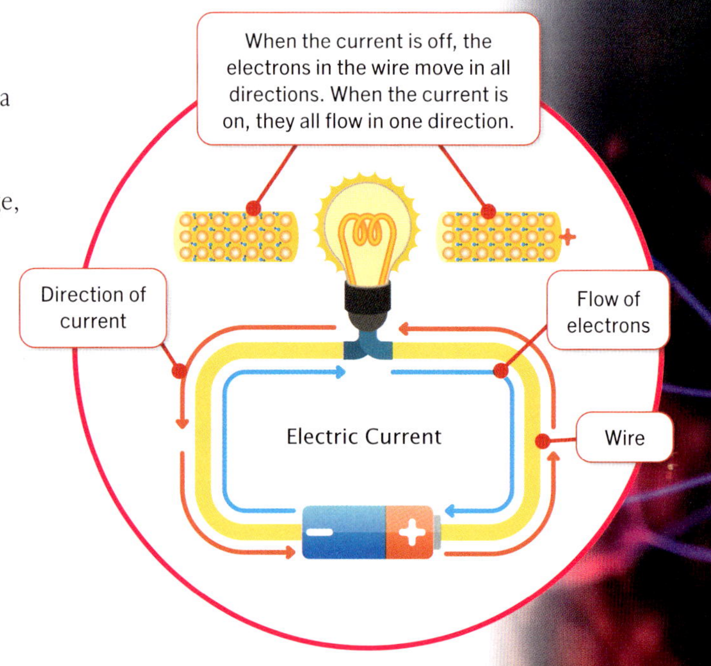

**HALL OF FAME**

**Luigi Galvani**
**1737–1798**

This Italian scientist investigated electric currents—by using frog legs! Galvani was an expert in muscles and nerves. He saw that the muscles in a dead frog's legs twitched when struck by an electrical spark. He thought this was due to a special kind of electricity called animal electricity, which was later disproved by the Italian physicist Alessandro Volta.



**DID YOU KNOW?** Electric current is measured in amperes, or amps. A current of 1 amp moves 6,240,000,000,000,000,000 electrons every second!

## AC and DC

There are two kinds of currents used by electrical systems. They are direct current (DC) and alternating current (AC). In DC, the electrons flow in one direction, like the water in a river. In AC, the electrons are constantly switching direction, moving forward and then back. Despite not going anywhere, AC still holds energy and is good for use in long-distance power cables. National-level electricity grids use AC, while car batteries and solar panels use DC.

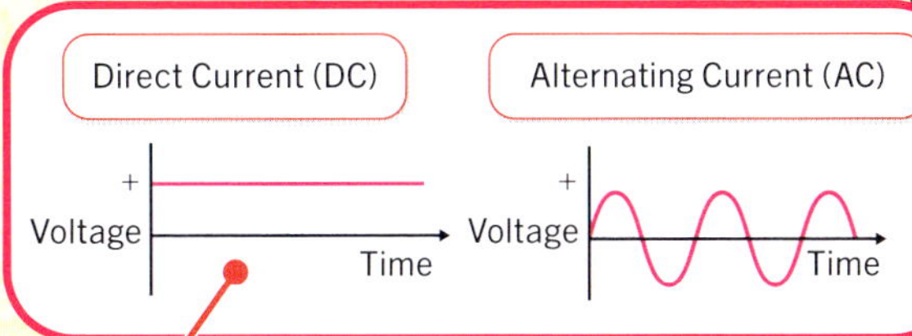


An electrical current is converted to DC when it is used to run devices such as computers and TVs.

This ball is filled with electrified gas. When an electric current flows through the gas, it leaves a trail of glowing plasma.

Plasma trails work a bit like a bolt of lightning, only they are much safer!

This person's hand is creating a path for the current carried by the positively charged plasma arcs to reach the negatively charged ground.

# Voltage

Just like anything that moves, an electric current needs a push to get going. This push is called the voltage, which is a measure of the difference in electrical charge. When the difference is large, the voltage is high and the current moves with great force. A high voltage is needed to get large currents moving.

If the voltage is high enough, it can push an electric current through anything, even air. This is what happens during a lightning strike.

## Danger

Electricity is dangerous. Its energy can burn the skin, damage internal organs, and even stop the heart from beating. High-voltage currents can hurt people who get too close—even if they don't touch the charged material. So, always be aware of warning signs posted near electrical equipment.

## Transformers

The voltage of an electric current is controlled by a transformer. Power plants make low-voltage electricity, which is transformed to a high voltage to be sent over a long distance. Before it enters homes, the electricity is reduced to a much lower, safer voltage once again.

Transformers are housed in electricity substations, which handle the power supply for a local area.



**DID YOU KNOW?** The loud thunder crack from lightning comes from the electricity making the air spread out so fast that it breaks the sound barrier.

HALL OF FAME

## Alessandro Volta
## 1745–1827

The word *volt* comes from the name of this Italian physicist. In the early 1800s, Alessandro Volta invented the first battery. He used piles of metal disks stacked with acid-soaked paper. These substances reacted with one another, creating a stream of electrons that flowed out of one end and into the other. A similar system is still used in many modern batteries.

# Circuits

Electric currents flow only through closed loops called circuits. A circuit connects a power supply to electrical devices and provides them with energy. Circuits can be controlled with a switch that closes the loop or cuts the power. When a switch is turned off, the connection between the wires is broken so the current cannot flow. When it is on, the circuit is complete and the current flows.

Light strings are a simple series circuit. There is one circuit passing through one light after another.

## In Parallel

Circuits can connect devices in parallel or in series. To the right is a parallel circuit in which each bulb has its own connection to the power supply. If one light bulb is disconnected, the other two will stay lit since current still flows through the other paths. The voltage is the same in each path of a parallel circuit, but there might be different currents depending on the resistance of each bulb.

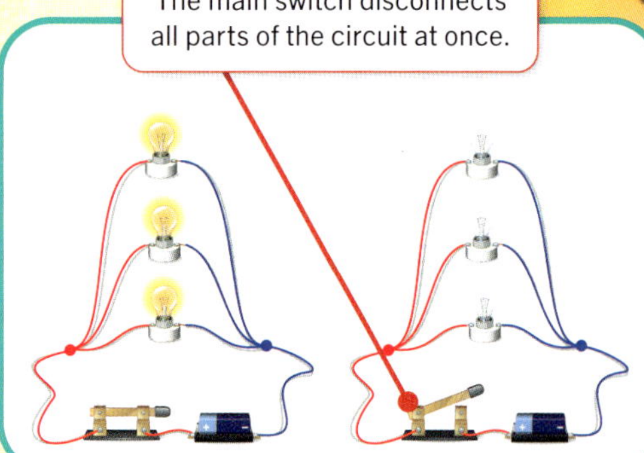

The main switch disconnects all parts of the circuit at once.

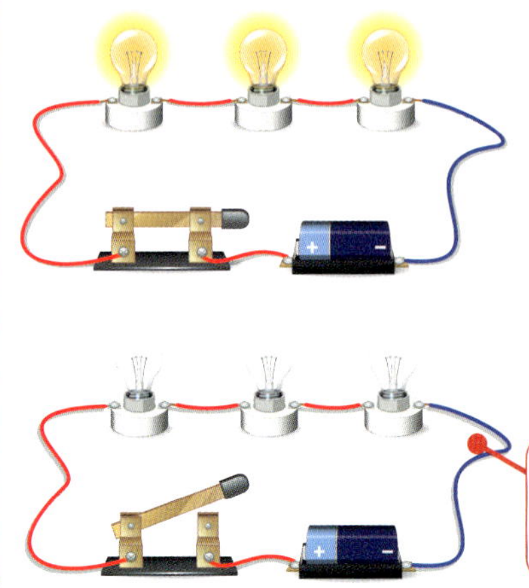

## In Series

These light bulbs are connected in series. They are in a single line on the same connection to the power supply. If the circuit is broken anywhere, all three lights will go out. There is only one path for the current, and the same current runs through every bulb.

This kind of circuit is easy to create, but it is not as useful as a parallel circuit. Most circuits in homes are parallel circuits.

**HALL OF FAME**

## Edith Clarke
### 1883–1959

Edith Clarke was the first woman to work as an electrical engineer in the United States. She later became the country's first female professor of electrical engineering. Clarke was an expert in the workings of the power grid and invented a system that made it easier to calculate the voltage, resistance, and other features of high-powered transmission cables.

**DID YOU KNOW?** The longest single length of electrical cable in the world is 3.3 miles (5.3 km) long. It connects a power station in Greenland to the capital city Nuuk.

# Electronics

Almost every modern electrical machine, from a washing machine to a phone, is electronic. While electricity works at large scales, with a current driving a motor or lighting a bulb, electronics work at a much smaller scale, with tiny currents and small numbers of electrons. Instead of large circuits, electronics use tiny ones, often etched into minute slices of a semiconductor material.

## Transistor

The transistor is an important electronic device that can work in two ways. It can take in a small current and use it to trigger the flow of a larger current. This is how a hearing aid amplifies a sound. It can also turn a current on and off thousands of times a second. This is central to how computers work. Groups of transistors linked together use electric currents to send lots of information very quickly back and forth within a computer.

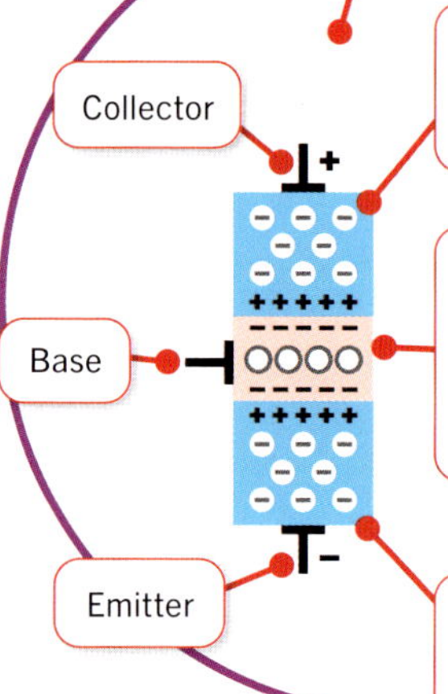

A transistor has at least three connections. Adding a small current to the base connection in the middle causes a larger current to flow between the collector and the emitter.

HALL OF FAME

**Esther M. Conwell**
**1922–2014**

Esther Conwell was an American physicist who discovered how electrons move through semiconductors. Without this breakthrough, the computers and other gadgets we use every day could not have been made! Conwell was the first woman to win the Edison Medal given for an outstanding career in the electrical sciences.

## Semiconductors

A semiconductor is a material that has properties somewhere between those of a conductor and an insulator. Most semiconductors are made from silicon, an element found in sand. How well a semiconductor conducts electricity can be changed by adding small amounts of other materials to it. An n-type (n for negative) semiconductor has extra electrons and conducts more easily. A p-type (p for positive) has fewer electrons and is less conductive. The two types of semiconductors can be joined to control the flow of current. Transistors and other components are made from semiconductors.

Silicon is shiny like a metal but cracks like a crystal.

A diode, such as an LED, is an electronic device that lets electric current flow through it only one way. The current flows from n-type to p-type silicon.

**This display screen is covered in tiny electronic light-emitting diodes (LEDs). Each LED creates one colored dot. Millions of dots create the full picture.**

**In an LED, electrons move between layers of silicon with different conductivity. As electrons move from n-type to p-type silicon, a tiny burst of light is emitted.**

**DID YOU KNOW?** More than one trillion semiconductor components are made each year.

# Understanding Matter and Energy

Modern physics can explain almost everything we observe about matter and energy. This knowledge helps us harness energy to heat our homes and run our devices. But there are still questions to be answered. In fact, we may understand only a small fraction of what there is to know about the energy and matter that exists in the universe. Emerging technologies are helping scientists better understand theoretical or newly discovered forms of matter and energy, such as dark matter.

## Dark Matter

Scientists have noticed something strange about the matter in our universe. Using telescopes, they have measured the matter in visible galaxies and have found that the mass of the known universe is greater than the total mass of the visible stars and galaxies. This extra matter that hasn't been detected is known as dark matter. Scientists are using extremely sensitive equipment to try to find evidence of this mysterious matter.

Dark matter detectors are deep underground to shield them from all other particles and radiation.

## Nuclear Energy

Nuclear power may play an important role in battling climate change. It harnesses the strong and weak nuclear forces to create a reliable source of energy. Some nuclear fuel can be reused over and over again, making it a renewable resource. However, some nuclear fuel cannot be reused, and the waste must be buried for a long time until it decays into safe material.

Lights from human cities lit by electrical power can easily be seen at night by astronauts aboard the ISS.

# Review and Reflect

Now that you've read about matter and energy, let's review what you've learned. Use the following questions to reflect on your newfound knowledge and integrate it with what you already knew.

## Check for Understanding

1. What happens to matter when it gets warmer? What happens when matter cools? *(See pg. 6)*

2. Describe protons, neutrons, and electrons. Where are they in an atom? *(See pp. 8–9)*

3. How are mass and weight measured? Why can an object's weight sometimes change while its mass stays the same? *(See pp. 10–11)*

4. How would a physicist define the term *work*? What unit is used to measure work? *(See pp. 12–13)*

5. What is the law of conservation of energy and mass? *(See pg. 14)*

6. Name and describe three ways thermal energy moves within and between substances. *(See pg. 16)*

7. How would you describe the relationship between speed and kinetic energy? *(See pg. 18)*

8. What is electrical potential energy? How is it created? How is it usually stored? *(See pg. 20)*

9. What form of energy creates sound? *(See pg. 22)*

10. What is a power rating? What unit is used to measure it? *(See pg. 24)*

11. What is radioactivity? How is it used to create power? *(See pp. 26–27)*

12. What is a laser? Where does the word *laser* come from? *(See pg. 30)*

13. What are conductors and insulators? Give one example of each. How are they alike and different? *(See pg. 32)*

14. How do electrons create a current? *(See pp. 34–35)*

15. Name and describe two types of circuits. *(See pg. 38)*

## Making Connections

1. Compare and contrast two of the following types of energy: kinetic, thermal, potential, electrical, sound, or chemical.

2. What are current and voltage? How do they relate to each other?

3. Choose three people described in the Hall of Fame sidebars. Explain how their work or discoveries are connected.

4. Imagine you wanted to find out how well five different materials conducted electricity, and you wanted to rank those materials from best conductor to worst conductor. What steps would you take to prepare and execute this experiment?

5. Choose a tool or concept described in the book, and provide an example of how it is used in real life.

## In Your Own Words

1. Which thing or concept described in this book would you like to know more about? What questions would you ask to learn more?

2. Which of the scientists or discoveries described in the Hall of Fame sidebars do you think is most relevant to your life? Why?

3. If the electrical concepts described in this book had never been discovered, how would your life be different? Would it be better or worse?

4. Can you imagine an invention that would use some of the matter and energy concepts described in this book? What would this invention be, and how would it be useful?

5. Imagine you have the opportunity to interview one of the people described in the Hall of Fame sidebars. What three questions would you ask?

# Glossary

**black hole** an object in space that is so dense that light cannot escape the pull of its gravity

**conduction** the movement of heat or electricity through a substance

**convection** the transfer of heat through a liquid or gas due to moving currents

**electric current** a flow of particles that carry an electric charge

**electricity** a form of energy caused by the flow of electrons

**electromagnetism** the force that works between charged objects

**energy** the ability to do work that can be stored and transferred in different ways

**engineer** a person who designs and builds machines and structures

**force** a push or pull that can change the movement or shape of an object

**gravity** a force of attraction between all objects that have mass

**insulator** a substance that does not conduct electricity or heat easily

**kinetic** relating to motion

**magnetism** the property of some materials, such as iron, to attract or repel similar materials

**nuclear fission** a process in which the nucleus of an atom splits into two smaller nuclei, releasing energy as it does so

**nuclear fusion** a reaction when two nuclei join together to form a single, bigger nucleus, releasing energy in the process

**nucleus** the central part of an atom, made up of protons and neutrons

**power** a measure of how fast work is being done and energy is being used

**quark** a type of subatomic particle from which protons and neutrons are made

**radiation** an electromagnetic wave or a stream of particles that comes from a radioactive source

**resistance** a measure of how much a substance blocks, or resists, the flow of electricity

**subatomic** smaller than an atom

**velocity** the measure of how far something travels over a set period of time and in a direction

**voltage** a measure of the force that pushes an electric current through a material

**work** a measure of how much energy is being used

## Read More

**Ball, Leo.** *Supersimple Physics (Supersimple).* New York: DK Publishing, 2021.

**Goldsworthy, Kaite.** *Electricity (The Beginner's Guide to Physics).* New York: Lightbox Learning Inc., 2024.

**Kehoe, Rachel.** *Nuclear Energy (Energy for the Future).* Lake Elmo, MN: Focus Readers, 2022.

**McKenzie, Precious.** *The Micro World of Atoms and Molecules (Micro Science).* North Mankato, MN: Capstone Press, 2022.

## Learn More Online

1. Go to **FactSurfer.com** or scan the QR code below.
2. Enter "**Matter & Energy**" into the search box.
3. Click on the cover of this book to see a list of websites.

# Index